# From Reviews of Valerie Gillies' Work

'This is the most visual poetry, with a clear sharp love of surface detail . . . for me, it is the imagery, served by quiet sound, which lingers longest in the mind.'

**Ian Stephen, *The Scotsman***

'I like the way in which these poems are rooted in the elemental world . . . the craft and the truth are at one.'

**Robert Nye, *The Times***

'A poet of unusual technical ability.'

**Shirley Toulson, *British Book News***

'. . . a fountain of knowledge about many things.'

**Helen Allan, *The Eildon Tree***

'Valerie Gillies will be familiar from her *Tweed Journey*, a key text in contemporary writing. Her more recent material is deft and luxurious.'

**S. B. Kelly, *Border Telegraph***

'. . . all the time I was there I was walking in your poem.'

**Ann Matheson, Biggar Public Art**

'In character as in landscape, Gillies' fresh eye for detail allows her some exquisite effects . . . From the most violent instincts and frenzied motion, her tone distils a curious impression of stillness and mystery.'

**Gerald Mangan, *The Scotsman***

'I would like one day to read Valerie Gillies' autobiography . . . These are the poems of a mature celebrant of love.'

**Clive Fisher, *Financial Times***

'. . . economy of technique allied to clarity of vision . . . establishes her as a distinctive voice in British poetry.'

**James Aitchison, *The Herald***

# The Lightning Tree

Valerie Gillies

© Valerie Gillies, 2002

Polygon
An imprint of Edinburgh University Press Ltd
22 George Square, Edinburgh

Typeset in Bembo by
Hewer Text Ltd, Edinburgh, and
printed and bound in Great Britain by
Creative Print & Design, Ebbw Vale, Wales

A CIP record for this book is
available from the British Library

ISBN 0 7486 6326 6 (paperback)

The right of Valerie Gillies
to be identified as author of this work
has been asserted in accordance with
the Copyright, Designs and Patents Act 1988.

The author wishes to acknowledge the support of the
Scottish Arts Council for the purpose of writing this book.

The Publisher acknowledges subsidy from

THE SCOTTISH ARTS COUNCIL

towards the publication of this volume.

for everyone at Maggie's Centre
with gratitude

# CONTENTS

# ACKNOWLEDGEMENTS

Thanks to the editors of the following magazines and anthologies where some of these poems were first published:

*Chapman*; *Scotia Review*; *New Writing Scotland*; *Oar* (Orkney); *Present Poets 1 and 2* (National Museums of Scotland); *The Shore Poets*; *Carmichael's Book*; *Trimontium Trumpet*; *The Eildon Tree*; *Poetry Scotland*; *Love for Love*; *The Jewel Box CD*.

# COMMISSIONS

Thanks to the commissioners of some of the poems:

Artlink Hospital Arts; Borders Festival; National Museums of Scotland; Scottish Borders Enterprise / Scottish Natural Heritage; City of Edinburgh Archaeologist and the City Art Centre; Fruitmarket Gallery; Morning Star Press; Edinburgh International Book Festival; Scottish Poetry Library; pocketbooks; Tweed Rivers Group; Forest Enterprise.

# Part 1

# A Lightning Print

Cloud-to-ground cracks its long spark,
it kills one in every six it strikes.

I break the lightning like a bell,
it goes around the outside of me,

it jumps the gap, it leaps,
I'm changed for ever.

My mouth is full of silver
and I can't even spit it out.

A whiff of smoke rises off my scalp,
scorchmarks on my soles,

the feet swivel round on my heels,
my back becomes my breast.

A photo of my surroundings
appears on my skin,

a glow around my hand.
I treasure life every day,

I love the lightning,
I walk out and I watch it.

# A Sonnet for Sorley

He went on climbing Cuillins with his wounded foot.
His flask broke at the summit but he drank the air.
He heard the bare rock-faces and the Bhasteir Tooth
Confirm what Gaelic verse has always said was there.

Beyond spire and splinter-peak, open out to view
Brown crag, green slope and dark-blue sea.
Then he saw hayfield and pasture empty too
And Europe slipping like frost-shattered scree.

On the main ridge in its semicircle
The curving crest of the pinnacle
Turns the echo travelling from Sgurr Alasdair.

His track of words will not melt and go
From the deep corries made of bleak gabbro.
In the company of mountains, he is everywhere.

## Beldorney Castle
*for the seventeenth-century poet, Sileas na Ceapaich*

When the sun warms the field
the moss issues a mist,
the Deveron's shallows yield
a stone that fills the fist.

A long drive over the Cabrach
almost into Strathbogie
in a hired car to her castle,
the fir flower of Beldorney.

What'll we say, Sileas,
if we meet at your old home,
'Let's ride abreast
and hear each other's poems?'

Our hostess, more than kind,
says, 'I know what it's like:
you talk about Sileas
as if you saw her last night.'

Though she's not here,
on painted walls we trace
a horseman's leg-greave,
a lutenist's hand and face,

a kilted matchstick man
with cap and claymore,
a highlander on the hill,
wildwood, baskethilted sword.

Here a woman spoke in tune
who could praise or keen.
In her room today
her song plays with the stream.

We can see through the trees
close by the waterside
the walled yard she watched
after her child died.

Standing at her window
recalls her three-year trance
to inspire her poetry
when she neither ate nor drank.

Daughter of the fifteenth chief,
she composed full strength
battle poems, night hymns,
reports of birth and death.

In her panelled room,
although she isn't here,
when Crisdean sings in Gaelic
the oaken walls have ears.

She made heroic songs
but the Jacobites lost all,
those Gordons are in Spain now.
As Conde de Mirasol,

in a castle like Beldorney
he is remembering his loss,
when the sun warms the field,
mist issues from the moss.

## Basking Adders

After rain, out come the adders
Sun-basking on a bank of earth
Below the hill they give their name to, Nathro,
We see great snakes dazzle the turf.
Brown mother-adder, short head and tail,
One long muscle with a copper eye
Glides forward, propelled by belly-scales
Each scale an oar to row her by

And on the sunny slope her viper-brood
The young of one year old entwine and coil
In running knots they loop the loop,
Beaded bronze wire soldered in spirals.
Sunlight twists in their skin, little stick-pins
Hold their spectators. They are transfixing
Us to adderstanes. We stand as close as we can,
The lucky amulet punctured by the fang.

# Ballad of the Wild Brown Hare

The scrub-oak trees have ears to hear
and every field has eyes to see
his long back and great hindlegs,
most marvellous beast that there can be.

He's made to stand on his four paws,
his eyes move round the sides of his head,
his neck is warm red docken leaf,
dark on his back as blackthorn hedge.

He likes both a hollow and a hill,
his coat is of the brown hareskin,
he brings the sun onto his back
for he loves to lie under the wind.

A hare on the edge of Ettrick Water
is sitting up with his ears laid back,
lost in watching the strong-flowing stream
he belongs to the bracken and the bank.

A good brown hare before hounds
enters the river and swims across,
he feels the surge where they swim too,
hot breath when they snap and snash.

His ears flatten at full speed,
he swerves and jinks and leaps a loop,
surprised to find himself so fast
the greyhounds yelp and overshoot.

On the stubble slope he runs uphill
till he can race over a rise
like the bird flying with the gale
he skims out of sight as he flies.

## The Hare's Form

where the hare rises
like the wind
over open space
follow him

going uphill
watch him leap
to break the trail
near his resting-place

in the boat-shaped
trodden pad
keeping his print
grounded

put a hand
into the form
to feel the warmth
in the earth

## Lepus

Sit tight. Flow into the ground
as if skin and bone are melting.
Get smaller as you're approached.
If that stone diminishes, it's you.

After a wet summer, when the cover
grows thick, sit in your own shape
till you're almost trodden on.
Move off, leaving your lair still warm.

In a dry summer, when the grass
is thin and sparse, and already
you've travelled far by night,
shift off out of slipping distance.

Hug the shoulder of a hill.
Go around to rest, circling
in the lee of the wind.
Bring the sun onto your back.

Weird being without feather or wing
lie out in the frost, live on
at the limits of the uplands,
wild hare folding into fog.

Be there in all the same places
you always are, Orion following
you across the sky fields.
Run on, lang lugs, take me with you.

## Runway Lights

where jets are taking off or landing
the wild hares teem

while noisy aircraft are taxiing round
hares cruise stiff-legged

near engines roaring like thunderclaps
they skip in the air

the hares who were here before we appeared
love the storm

the hares who can feel our footfall vibrate
they like the airport

they race alongside at take-off
trying to overtake

they run in the passengers' sight
we watch them

— cleft lips, fluffed cheeks, side-set eyes —
they watch us

each individual varies in colour and shape
hares vary as humans do

racing for the sun-gates, no time to pass
the dew-hoppers run

through a point separating every here from there
the hares lead the way

## Two Birds

two birds on my head
one was in the leafy den
I was sitting so still
the short-sighted wren
landed in my hair
light as a blessing

the other on the hill
the puppy chasing a fledgling
the old crow struck my crown
cuffed me with claws
drawing blood in a graze
heavy as a curse

# Carnyx Blarnyx
*for John Kenny*

a boar's head blows in
with a wooden tongue
moved by springs
in sheet-bronze

rattles his jaws
shows his scars
bristles with tusks
the brazen boar

gives his brassy bray
red over yellow
beneath our feet
the ground bellows

on shifting slopes
the forests wave
the boar is near
both fast and brave

the river runs
by ridgeback hill
his flying shadow
just visible

the valley sounds
mouth open so
great time can come
small time can go

# Singing the Storm
*for Savourna Stevenson*

I'll never arrive
on moving land
in shifting skies
I need the map
of another planet

No valley or hill
no roads, no cars
in a white shell
I'm hearing the sea
who's hidden the stars?

Snow seeks a form
a flock of ice
runs in the storm
a dark shepherd
whistles and drives

Someone's going by
in the wind
where the wayward
bird dies
and the cold begins

It ends on a note
gusty and hollow
I take off
my coat
for a pillow

Singing the storm
going to sleep
now I can dream
it's getting warm
beneath the sheets

I go out through my smile
I follow the snow
mile after mile
I go with
the wind and snowdrift

## In the Trail of the Wind

Winter midnight
it's been snowing
and the wind's blowing

the horse flings up his head
thoroughbred
born to carry a rider
clear of the fray
he's away

alone in the wild wind
Ericstane cantering
out there
through two gates
jumps the cattlegrid
thunders louder
along the lochside
hoofprints in ice
black script on white

dark horse in a white night
galloping to the head of the valley
all the way

over the burn
up the back of the farm
by the old tower
where Sir Simon Fraser
rode out to meet
the same fate as the Wallace

a great charger riderless
under the old beech trees
under the high heronry
he circles
with his New Zealand rug on squint
he flaps longlegged night heron

he has run two miles through the hills
at midnight
now he spooks at everything
at something in the wind
so close
you just can't see it
ghosting his moonlight flit

## Suave Dancer

The starved lightning chose Suave Dancer,
famous racehorse in his paddock outside Melbourne,
the stallion among the mares, siring dreams,

   the current travels through his hooves.

The shadow of a hungry bird falls on his face.
Race the horse of the sky against the horse of the earth,
the traveller in the wind is lost in the morning

   before the sacrifice of a colt to the year.

The pure-bred horses see him for a long time.
Under the horse-tree of his veins the stallion stands
in his own shade and the lightning lifts a horse's skull

   and other omens are on the way.

## Scottish Eclipse
*for Sudeep Sen*

Are you watching this clear night,
making out the curved edge
of the shadow crossing the moon's disc?
It begins like a bruise, gives her a keeker.

The taxi driver pulls over to the kerb
and we sit gazing together,
clap hands and call out
to help her shrug off the shade.

But the stars grow bigger, stronger,
outshine her. She's not completely gone.
Into the shadow she's stolen
my year in Manasa Gangotri

and she's hidden away
Sudeep's month in Scotland:
in each particular place
one lunar eclipse or two every year.

The moon is always presenting
the same face to earth;
now she glides out to watch us
again, like a silvery third party.

# Ivor Gurney at Bangour

*Ivor Gurney, poet. With Gloucesters in France, 1916. Gassed near Passchendaele; sent to Bangour War Hospital, autumn 1917. Died, London asylum, 1937. Complete poems published, 1954.*

It's always that spooky light in November,
the winter lightlessness. He liked that too,
Ivor, an inmate here, a trench-companion.

The hospital had its own station then.
Three short blasts on the steam hooter to say
the ambulance train was arriving in darkness.

Stretcher-bearers at the shed with lamps
lit. Alerted by telegram, *300 tonight.*
Some sitting, some lying prone, fever cases,

or with gassing and shellshock. Like Ivor.
Tents for the thousands of angry amputees.
Tree-stumps in the leaf-litter woods,

plane and lathe in the peg-leg workshop,
a basket wheelchair with a headlamp. Now
it's tossed out on the skip. Under floorboards

lie a stack of glass negatives, medical photos
of head injuries, warriors' faces blown away.
Birch trees erupt through the station platform.

## St Fillan's Crook

A stranger to its native strath,
the tall foreigner, the *coygerach*
was at the crowning of our kings,
raised the crest of all bright things.

Its keeper went to eastern Canada,
he carried the crook, the nomad
to use its crystal as a cattle cure.
Where it dips, the water's pure.

From Canadian forests, settlers sent
the wanderer back into its element,
silver stripes crossing the Atlantic.
The brightness is inside the relic.

# I am Speaking to my Saint

I am speaking to my saint
in the dark and in the day
in months of light and shade
    Fillan my love

the frost never touches you
the sun stands still for you
the earth rises under you
    your shadow heals

your bell flies in the day
it goes ringing all the way
to one named for our lady
    curing her fever

saint of the bronze bell
saint of the holy pool
saint of the silver crook
    come to my child

saint of the shining hand
saint of the armbone
saint of the healing stones
    help cure her

saint of the serried hills
saint of Glendochart's cell
in your chapel of marvels
    take away her pain

saint of the mountain pass
saint of the curved staff
a riverbend around the lass
    keep her well

in the deep pool she's dipping
give grace to the living
on your rock she's landing
    Fillan my love

breathe life into her mouth
all the cold will go out
of the water that you touch
    Fillan, see my Mairi

## The Routing Well

When the Routing Well breathes out
it touches you by word of mouth:
half-hidden in the underwood
it utters the primordial word.

Eight miles inland, it's said
to warn you of rough times ahead.
A rumbling noise precedes
high winds, and spills their secrets.

> *The rush of the rye*
> *the raw of the root*
> *the rev of the race*
> *will raise the roof!*

Where the sea puts in messages
from the far storm to the beaches,
here fathoms deep down below
coal rooms and shafts are hollow,

faults and fractures in an area
like a Roman amphitheatre
where wild beasts kept underground
roar and pace round and around.

> *the ring of the ruff*
> *the ruse of the rhyme*
> *the rove of the ray*
> *will rouse the rout!*

Storms turn up hydraulic pressure
on air and water in the fissure,
through a throaty press of rock
new frequencies begin to knock,

reverberate, a child gurgling,
the root of a tongue gargling,
you know it's speech of some kind
breaking through to send a sign.

*the row of the riff*
*the roar of the reverb*
*all resound one word*
*the word is out — 'rout!'*

# The Gladsmuir Fireball

Over this barren ridge
pared of its turf
the thunderstorm sways.
The school stands in its way.

Two boys in an attic room
— sent to fetch books —
hear a buzzing noise
and see a spinning fuzz

come through the skylight,
golden red in colour.
What's rolling?
What's glowing?

Round, football-size,
it flutters over their heads
about six feet off the ground
going straight down

the length of the room
with no effect on the boys
except for a tingle there
as it passes over their hair

at the rate of a fast run
over one then the other.
A ball-lightning sphere
on a trip through the air.

They could grab it easily
but it strikes the wall
with a bang like a meteor.
It spatters into streamers,

burning with a sulphur smell.
It's only now they know
they're seeing something strange
and dangerous.

Lightning does strike twice.
A side-flash current flows in
and levels the schoolhouse
in smoke and dustcloud.

In the other room
the schoolmaster and children
stunned, lie senseless
beneath tables and benches,

while the two whose heads
it hovered over
as the travelling spark
are gazing at its mark.

Their eyes retain its stroke.
Today a black cloud still
terrifies the whole school,
one clap scatters the little troop.

# Dog Stone, Glen Lyon

Dog Stone
knit my bone

tether-stake
tie my fate

old tent-peg
move your head

dog hook
take a look

rocky jaw
give me a paw

stony ground
turn my life around

stripy stem
bring me here again

brindle granite
speed the planet

Dog Stone
lucky knucklebone

# Part 2

# Vision of Tinto Hill

i) *'You may experience some discomfort'*

a needle test
into my left breast
I see flame
on the beacon cairn
needling the fiery pap
on Tintock-tap


ii) *'performing the tests, getting the results'*

a small needle
into the smooth undulating billowy hill
a dark nipple
on the mass of bright flesh-coloured rock

the perfect cone
where screes slide down the long slopes
the bare zone
grows as the hill wears away

tethering
the breast to the place of fire
weathering
each rock in its own way

## Golden Breast

'Say goodbye to your breast,' she said,
'for tomorrow it will be gone.'

So I walked far into the hills.
I opened my shirt,
the sun set on my breast.

Next day, the tissue
the surgeon cut
and the pathologist placed
between slides,
that wasn't the golden breast
on the hill
in a place where light stays.

## Cool Cap

You couldn't have a serious conversation
with any one who looks like me
under the cool cap during chemotherapy.

A cobalt-blue two-layered helmet
like a Woman-in-the-Wind biker wears,
the cap comes out of the freezer. Icecrust on it.

When the great wave comes crashing
and the chemicals rush to my scalp
the cap stops my hair falling out.

The freezing layer caps the globe.
I'm under the permafrost, it's preserving
this nomad woman with her six horses.

Here's my needle tattoo on kidskin, my weird
colour hair, my strange crescent headgear.
Let in today's air, I melt away,

fading out the derbyday trampling beat
of those wild gallops on the high plateau,
the grip of this hard hat thawing.

# The Charmstone

Rock crystal, a clear quartz.
Ice-like, hope freezes
in one of the living stones.

Dipped in drinking water to protect
against disease, it transfuses
a bowlful with its gleam.

The charmstone radiates itself. Strange,
how it comes up from the earth
but lets light pass through it.

Last century they laughed at it.
The healing charm of a thousand years
was a tear running down skin.

When a hand holds the stone,
human touch encloses a white breath.
It is like us, made of star stuff.

The glass doctor comes to cure
in a small burst of energy,
the first beam of radiation therapy.

## Charms against Ill

If you fear each dream's new shape
Take a pebble that waves perforate
String it by a piece of tape

Hang it on your bedpost, keep
Away the nightmare from your sleep.
Mare stone washed up by the sea,

Driftseeds the warm currents bore
Fetch up on our western shores,
You hear these have healed before.

Bring the charmstone, hogback crystal,
Atomic structure of the mineral,
Touch it and it is medicinal.

Catch your stone in water or air
Make it float in space there
Light glints off it while you stare

To look through its transparency.
It may let you see the stray
Danger you dread coming your way.

Now set free a hidden secret,
The thunderflash flint arrowhead
Thrown up in storms to be an amulet.

## Marble

Some terrible steelie lofted from space,
a meteor might shatter the glassy ocean . . .
But not now you've found my marble.
You knew it was mine, brought it in for me.
I see it is my best blue alley,
the joy of a favourite
click in a pocket.

When friends knuckled down for a game
played with the boys from the farms,
this was a shooter, out to capture
their aggies, their bulleys or bumboozers,
immies or mibs, milkies or twofers.

I cupped them in my palms;
chinas and clays, transparent clearies,
clambroths like chowder, zulus or zebras,
custards and daubs, glassies and glimmers,
playing chasey with cat's-eyes and swirls,
wherever spun-glass might
lure us with light.

We were sharpshooters at bounce eye,
flicked a taw between thumb and forefinger,
our circle etched with a stick in the soil.
We kept a galaxy in a marble-bag,
stardust destined to roll in the dirt.

This one lay out on the moor, a sphere
filled with a glittering landscape.
A comet shaping the globe,
bringer of light and laughter,
a dream world I hold in my hand,
my blue marble again
no beginning or end.

## Snow Globe

A child's snow globe
hides in the back of a drawer
I pick up the dome
and storm clouds the scene
with silver
flitter

There's a blue field
with a boy on a sled
snowflakes blowing
all around him, obscuring
the catchall
bauble

If I could prolong
the time it takes the snow
to fall,
it would go
at a slower rate
tight seal
unreal

Chances are
he's causing a few
snowstorms himself
around the world
blizzard-weight
crystal-shake

# Five Poems at Fifty

## 1 The Snipe

Eyeing everything carefully, waiting my turn
to switchback in a long queue of the cancer clinic,
I look out to the rushy fields and wet upland moors
where I found this barred snipe's feather
I'm carrying in a pocket. Erratic

snipe fly crazily but know
how to jink out of danger
when they are flushed, the birds go
rising and zigzagging away
twisting and turning with hoarse calls.

At the gun-barrel end
of the biopsy instrument
I hear snipe drumming and bleating
as the air-stream rushes past their tail feathers
jinking and flying for their striped lives.

It's their feathers that give out a plaintive sound,
surprising me over a long distance.
Later I stare at my feather
at every bold cream and brown bar
seeing it for the first time.

## 2 How to Transcend

It can be any one of us. How to
pass over limits, rise above
needles in the hand
finding a port in a vein?

How to get over
the prepping with marker pens,
not writing but being written on?

How to go beyond
one arm dangling,
the bird-flight pectoral
too weak to bring forward?

The heart feathering
through my breast,
for now, anyway,
I lift a
     trailing
         wing
            and
               fly

### 3 Fantail

after the sparrowhawk
attack
the talon-marks show
a puncture-wound
below each wing
if the dove is quiet
if she's calm
bird-flesh heals fast

## 4 Mairi Messenger

Rainclouds were clotting cold and wet
when an angel arrived off the island plane
appearing at the foot of my bed in the ward
with the light on her body
she carried windblown from Orkney

a halo of pure far places
with her sea-grey penetrating eyes
a strand of freckles across her face
and her hair salt-blonde
from swimming with Papa Westray seals.

## 5 Red Poll
*for Glyn Jarvis*

Looking for cup-and-ring markings
on the exposed faces of the outcrops
at Dall, on the south shore of Loch Tay,
I search in low sun and a spot of rain,
good conditions for making them out.

Is that one? A groove filled with moss.
And this? A pecked ring of lichen
round a simple cup? I can't be sure,
taking a bearing northwards to Ben Lawers,
the loch lying in its deep hollow below.

There, across the loch, is the other shore,
the side where I climbed the ben, saw the ridge,
spoke to the farmer who tried to cut rock art
with a bit and brace; he said it took for ever.
Now I'm on this shore, rest on this rock-sheet.

Scrutinising its silver-grey flanks, I hear
hooves. Slab-sided, with a gapped ring
in his nose, the biggest Red Poll bull
I've ever seen is on the slope just above,
watching me intently. I stay quiet,

at a hundred metres from the gate.
He wanders downhill alongside me
till he reaches an opening in the fence
and crosses through into the next field. Animal
guardian of this site, show me the calm shore.

## A Few Haiku

out comes the sun
wind blows up over the hill
— kite flying a boy


sometimes forgetting
put his tea on the table
beside the others


wet to our skins
our black umbrella waving
no taxi stops


all night long
moon kept coming in and out
no-one lost the place


storm is fishing with
the thunder and lightning fly
black with an orange streak


Norman Iain Sorley George
Scalpay Lewis Raasay Hoy
each poet an island


sit on the platform
buoyed up on bare boards
— palomino horse

# Part 3

## The Space between Us

In his glen one song always goes on air
Round the lip of Corrie Vanoch, where I first heard it.
I see him everywhere I look, a moving figure,
Spring-heeled he walks the slopes, leaps the stream,
And he speaks from the well-head of Tobar a' Chinn.

When I follow the pass upwards towards Monega,
Time is running by me with a sleety kiss
And a footprint appears in new snow beside mine.
If I turn round suddenly in the fields of his farm
His gaunt good looks are easily seen on Craig Soilleur.

Over the high ridge of Cuingard I hear the storm
Eddy through cliff and cleft like a windpipe,
While his song keeps on coming, a torrent
That never stops flowing through the ravine.
The space between us takes shape where he calls
On love, in the breezeway of Glen Isla's sonic seam.

# Island of Canna

*i) Compass Hill*

the rocks themselves are magnetic
— into the pull of the hill
the needle goes berserk


*ii) After the Storm*

in the Sound of Canna
a big swell
resounds for days and nights


*iii) Maeve*

on the cliff-edge against a gale force 7
she takes an airbath in a starshape
nothing to hold her back

# Maeve in Manhattan

She's the sibyl of silver
the prophet of platinum
techno diva in titanium
she's the goldsmith girl

long nights in the studio
welding at a workbench
going gem-cutting
with jewellers in Jaipur

she's enamelling in India
powder-coating spun copper
like a Kawasaki motorbike
she's metalworking in Manila

turns her lathe in typhoons
drives to live volcanoes
scuba-dives to corals
the goldsmith girl

closes vice and clamp
zaps her Zag toolbox
on files and fretsaws
silver scrap and ring shanks

the girl comes and goes
with her fibre-optic neckpiece
flashing stellar galaxies
pricing precious metals

she rollerblades to work
creating catwalk jewellery
kinky kinetic
slinky prophetic

alien abduction
astral seduction
starry nights in gold and steel
the goldsmith girl

## Shellycoat

On the site of the new docks, his rock was blown up.
People are asking, *Ah, who's the odd-looking one,*
*the spirit of the waters with a skin of shells?*

Oysters the size of a man's fist, woven into his hair
— those flowing fronds of bootlace weed — make
a strange clattering when he tosses with the surge.

He lives his life in other creatures' armour
like a hermit crab. He lights up the bay, filling
its big space with the clash of jingling mussels.

If the tide's coming in, yes, he'll have some of it
while he's looking for his standout rock. Masked
furrows on his head resemble a human face,

a carapace with three lobes between the eyes.
He likes singing into the mirror of a salty gully,
mouth tentacles rim his lips like burst bubblegum.

He's not the boy in the pool you want to swim with.
That cloudy brow has come from somewhere deep
and humans prey on him if they can break his shell.

He wears barnacle-encrusted everything, he's poured
into frothy neck-ruffs, decorated with seed pearls.
In his glitzy garb he shimmies up beside the reef

with brittlestar arms, shines a ring of blue warts
on soft coral fingers held out towards the light,
the heart urchin in his holdfast belt of kelp.

Tonight he'll turn up head-to-toe in shells
and brew a storm of bubbling bass, he'll remind us
this was once sea, and could be so again.

# From Inscriptions across Scotland

## Quick Water

*Text in bronze, Galloway Forest Park, with sculptor Jake Harvey*

Palfern springs between alder trees
turns back to the wind at Tonderghie
down Grey Mare's Tail and Clugie Linn
falls pierce the mountain with their din
through a strip for cattle, Carseveige Burn
then the chattering one, the little Louran
along Barhoise with its field of thistles
the yellow clearing where Blairbuis rustles.

In paradise, Bargaly hazelwood
grow nut and leafy branch and root.
Under Bardrochwood, field at the bridge
round Kirroughtrie's brindle ridge
between Muirfad Flow's long marsh
and the rich loop of Meikle Carse
clear Palnure, stream of the yew tree
winds to the fish-trap Cruives o Cree.

52

## Tweed's Well

*Text in stone, with sculptor Fly Freeman, at the source of the River Tweed*

This moor is an open hand,
    The palm lined with streams.
In winter, on the frozen land,
    Tweed's Well shows up as green.

In summer when the upland dries
    The source is flowing free
A clear spring will always rise
    While Tweed runs to the sea.

## Ballad of Leaderfoot
*for Liz Niven*

*Text in stone, with sculptor Garry Fay, Leaderfoot*

The river runs from west to east
    roads south to north
from bank to bank three bridges span
    three centuries' worth

before these the Fly-boat Brae
    led down to its ferry
near the ghost-line of the Roman way
    on the outward journey

salmon sandstone pillars rise
    above Leaderfoot
the meeting of two singing streams
    by leafy Ravenswood

builders pay attention to the piers
    so the arch can spring
taking you far from what you see
    to what you're not yet seeing

for when the Tweed is running high
    from wintry moor and moss
old Drygrange Bridge is standing here
    to carry you across

## The Glide

*Text in bronze, with sculptor Denys Mitchell, Coldstream*

Near the ford, the crossing-place
for invading armies from either land

two nations marry like runaways
while the bridge links five spans.

Here fishermen cast march brown,
blue charm and silver stoat

over long deep pools, down
through The Glide, The Otter Stones.

A high walk has a handhold for you
where people meet and talk,

watch hills like waves, veined
with snow, Cheviot's flat top

floating above the floodplain,
the rich soil of Lees Haugh.

# The Big Bend of the Tweed

flowing away from you flowing towards you

## Bridge to the Beyond

sandstone piers
stand out
floating on woolsacks
— river's low, look out for them —
wet, set hard as concrete

pointed cutwaters
part the current
the humpie brig's parapets
are borne on a rising course
across the deep channel

cylinders of air
along the great arches
— o those voids
through hollow spandrels
are the eyes of the bridge

## The Sitooterie

a little way
from house or school
is the hidden hut
at a distance from it all

a log cabin
built of douglas fir
longlasting
here or elsewhere

you make a stay
go on retreat
where you look for shade
beneath a leaf

heat or cold
set no limit
for hand-cut timber
not a nail in it

the bluetit nests
in the crabapple tree
a butterfly sunning
takes time to be

with tap and patter
the wind picks up
rain pelts the roof
runs in the water butt

trace a raindrop
with your finger
you follow on foot
two great rivers

stand in the doorway
looking out
— step towards the world
or back into the hut?

a passing blackbird
sees you sitting still
taking sanctuary in
the sound of the hut's bell

— who's coming by
to find a bit of time?
the door is standing open
a hut's a state of mind

## Girl in the Yard

What is she supposed to do?
She helps in the yard, mucks out,
takes her turn with his brothers

feeding the herd. Filches a jacket
off a scarecrow for him. No need,
he is cured hide already.

Cuts pigs with him. Herds
at sales, rides a wild pony for him
in front of sharp dealers.

They travel to the mart together,
drive the cattle-truck, sing
*Take me back to the Black Hills* . . .

Wears her cap at his angle.
Copies his whistle. Bids
for cockerels. His tomboy

milks cows alongside him
in the long byre. Walks with him
as his look-alike. Saw-partners

draw the two-handed saw
ripping a kerf, each move
deepening the groove in logs.

What is she supposed to be?
His brothers turn the yard-hose
on her shirt cut from his cloth.

## Coomlees Farm
*for Eck's birthday*

Coomlees is on the slope, the windless side
of the valley, it lies in the lee of the coomb.
No matter what breeze is rustling through

the farm puts out that sense of calm
like a sound you've heard before, it fits
with your breath. Snipe are drumming

and the collies bark where hills are rising
each with its crest above the river's curve.
It's just here, at the edge of the beech trees

you hear it and slow down in the steading
with the fifteen-cow byre, lost acres and a bank
of the Tweed. Moss and rain eat away the name

on a wooden sign nailed to the tree-trunk, each
letter of Coomlees washed out but two: *om*, it says,
is this way, into the cosmos of all tones.

★

A sump-breaker track leads you to the deep,
to the dark, to the trees' rustle-and-slash
scything around whinstone house and byre.

Wooden planks flap from the hay-shed, gape
through metal sheets, patched 1940s adverts.
Batons hang over the eaves, tarnished fingernails.

The house has slipped a good few slates and the damp
stains through as you'll see inside. The front porch
is a broad brown cave in the roots of great beeches.

61

Woodlined gloom. You grow used to the treacle-dim
of dense leaves outside, the old rose-bubble wallpapers,
a carpet of beechmast matted indoors in twilight.

Rust-solid, the ochre bath is a dried stream-bottom.
The boys' room holds a hundred orange cartridge cases
on wooden shelves. Their beds sag under old quilts.

The back door's rotted through, sills are bare of paint.
The wife works in a kitchen with a window smaller
than any in the byre, it's her porthole to green waves.

That's farmers for you, they look after the field
first, the house second, all for the earthy round
where every mark grows manifold in furrows.

★

Not just a human home, on your way outside
you pass three Silkie bantams, moving white meringues
with red combs. Dod brought them for his mother.

An ancient lame turkey is no-one's dinner.
Eight white geese pace in from the grassy fields,
flush a rat running out of feedstuffs. Lambs follow

like dogs. And all the time the Tweed is harping
between banks of white shingle pebbles, every
wave form is the same flowing round the stone

in the spawning stretch for great salmon
who were spawned themselves at this bend.
No one can take them from here

nor can you bring away anything but
an inner thought of the white strand, one field
growing reeds, your stay in a sounding place.

★

62

By the cobbled *o* traced at the horse-mill,
by the midden *m* infilling the earthwork,
a young horn seems a stump beneath fur

and living forms lying behind every growth
lean down low in Coomlees' core.
A hollow scooped out by wind and ice

comes closest to how a place sounds
and you can recognise the ring to it
by the way your whole body is resonating.

Maybe you experience on a Monday in Coomlees
a slow humming from the numinous coomb,
one voice, one landform, chanting an audible *om* . . .

## Burn the Wind

When will they canter to the gate again
young calves and heifers, to rub hides

on our hands, nuzzle us with grassy
breath, frolic away over the slope?

If we're looking for an answer
the silent pasture gives us one

the smoke of the year's holocaust rises
the totem beasts burn.

# Reeds

I pull tall reeds for a child to take
from the mud shores of the Mugdrum
gathering a handful of cuts, razor nicks
        lacerating finger and thumb.

Early this wintry morning we spread
our hands in the dew of the grass
on our way out of the reedbed
        from estuary to terrace.

What Virgil did once for Dante
when he washed his face with dew
and plucked a reed belt for purgatory
        up ahead, we do too.

Reeds we bring from the tide
spring from a new root
they wave by a child's side
        move with a human foot

and tall as the sharp sea rush
long shadows cut out on our right
two men walking close by us
        on the shoreline of light.

## Greylag Language

rangangangang
quahg gegegegeg
spring lingerer
cackles in the leas
pale forewings
rising beating
white and grey
flock flies
orange ring-eye
bent pinion
straight-line
grey
honk
goss
aang
claik
gandra

rangan angang
quahg gegegegeg
lagging behind
grazes fieldgrass
slow wingbeat
up into the air
takes wing
as one bird
tucks away feet
feather fin
skein
lag-goose
hansa
gwdd
aang
quink
gandra

gos

## Corbie
*for Jake Harvey*

frae raen nest heuch
on the craig o the cliff
tummlin he flees
tapsalteerie
an janners tae the lift
*'bruch . . . bruch!'*

## Cliff Face

brinkwoman
   come close to the edge —
      I see you now for the first time
         your head in profile —

there you are
   the *cailleach* of the crag staring out
      cliff face, mother mountain
         on wild Craigencallie you

totem-rock
   seen from one side only
      geoglyph weathered in granite
         bare boss with white eyes of quartz

your ice-shuttle
   freezes the fall, the source
      of origin, out of it a head emerges
         that won't die, was never born

your head stacked
   high with scalps of peat
      a woman's face clearly visible
         a sign embedded in the rock

beak of stone
   look down from your precipice
      your hill haunted by ravens
         on their rock-ledge breeding-place

a black honeybee hums
   among the creeping thistle
      girls tell you their secrets at night
         the rocking stone rocks on your summit —

you turn into
    so many forgotten faces alive
        in the head up there on the mountain
            countless faces grin, cry, speak —

from far below
    a whistling wind threads through
        the Pin Rock, your crag needle
            — who can look you in the eye

that diamond of spar?
    see me, I am your progeny —
        why is half your face left out?
            — the other half is mine

# Part 4

# The Wraith Outdoors

*a sequence for the Cowie of Goranberry*

This is the story of the cowie, or banshee, who haunted the farm of Goranberry, near Hermitage Castle in Liddesdale, about 1800. Curiously similar to the Highland and Irish tradition, the Cowie followed a certain family native to the area, and gave warning of events to come. In particular, she forecast the drowning of her favourite, Adam Elliot, while he was crossing the ford of Hermitage Water on a stormy night.

The name 'cowie' is of obscure origin, probably from the Scots *cow*, 'an object of terror', but it may derive ultimately from the Gaelic *cumha*, 'keening, lament'. A. Jeffrey in his *History of Roxburghshire* writes in 1864 that 'It is not said that ever the cowie was actually seen . . . only heard.'

This poem-sequence conjures up that spirit of wild places. When the cowie sounds her banshee wail, she wakes up the *Panchamahasabdha* — the five great sounds.

73

## 1 Echo Location

Who has a neck like Hawk Hass?
Who's breasted like Maiden Paps?

Who yells in the Routing Burn?
Who cries on Reedy Edge?

Who bites with Carlin Tooth?
Who laps up Tongue Burn?

Who's wrapped in Cloak Knowe?
Who's the colour of Roan Fell Flow?

Who shines on Starcleuch Edge?
Who splashes her Burnfoot?

Who looks out from Watch Hill?
Who lifts her Cauldcleuch Head?

Who rouses the echo of Din Fell?
Who wails in Windy Gowl?

## 2 Poor Cowie

The howl-yowl girl, the frock in a mist,
her thrills blast out of nowhere,
she pushes the sonic envelope.

That girl translates to grief.
She gets weird in ripped gowns
exposing mosses and lichens.

She just walks on set
and goes for it, a spook-out stormer
calling his name without an answer.

She knows where to hang out,
who to see, plays with spectres.
He crackles with her static.

Her voice through a shiny hollow
rocks the valley. Gleaming alloy,
her hair with the birdshit highlights.

She's a howl without its wolf
she's a bark without its deer
the wind in a snipe's tail-feathers.

She hurls him towards a precipice
with a drop he's happy to take,
escapes into her own sound with him.

## 3 The Banshee is Back

The eddy wind is blowing
   It is eerie, it is eldritch
Where the wintry spate is flowing
   Suddenly through sike and ditch.

Swift as squall from gully
   In the stripe of the wind I leap
Behind the hill, in the face of the pass
   In front of the bare steep.

In the shadow of my look
   Where you can't see me yet
I saw you back to back with rocks
   On the riverbed without a breath.

You shiver though you aren't cold,
   You're setting out, even so.
I am the cowie, wild wirricow to call
   My forecast of your forego!

I try to speak, *whillelew,*
   I hear these weird cries pierce
The ululating *wirricoo*
   The force of the upcurrent's shriek.

Hidden in the cleugh, inside the seam
   Of the gorge-mouth I sound.
Spindrift passing over the ravine,
   My feet don't touch the ground.

Listen with thumping heart
   To the loud voice late on the hill.
Who's shifting ground after dark?
   Someone who's with you still.

## 4 Liddesdale Lament

The river runs among boulders
    Round about
His byres and fields. He hears her shout
Split the water over his shoulders.

An undertow tugs harder than the onrush.
    She's foretold
He'll fall from the saddle. She drones in the cold
Above the ford, she is the shaman in the bushes.

He is living with the unknown. Nearer than life,
    Between her ears
He is hearing what she hears:
Not his human, but his phantom wife.

The closer he looks, the more he'll see.
    Eyes stare
From her soluble face, the more blurred
They become, the more indelible they'll be.

## 5 The Cowie of the Roof-Rack

The storm came on
and she was coming on strong.
We'd left the metal roof-rack up

after taking rubbish to the tip.
As we drove along
the wind whistled through

and let the rails speak.
I knew what the sound was
but not who it was for.

*wow! wirricow*      *hai! whillelew*
who else      but the cowie
*hoo! ululu*      keening

waff wanhap      waith waverand
fey token      fanton foregang
bone crone      *oooo oo* drone

*wheeple whauple*      weird wife
wake the dead      stun the living
*dowie cowie*      it's no cannie

her *boo-hoo*      speeds up and soars
the wailing murmur      of unearthly music
no-one likes      to hear it

# The Lightning Tree at Duartbeg

Birch and hazel trees surround it, there's a taller ash nearby,
but it's the contorted twisted oak that attracts the lightning.
At a stroke, electricity in a frenzy smacks into it,
kindling the split second between bolt and thunder.

The crest already falling, tottering to the left, a spattering
of outstretched twigs hurl headlong earthwards, the pressing
faces of moss and lichen are blasted off the trunk. Four long
roots in earth blow up, the ground takes on a positive
    charge.

A high-voltage pulse running down inside vaporises sap,
strips leaves, rocks the forest; a flying bomb goes off. Boughs
fling themselves apart. A spiral scar winds round the oak,
cracked on its axis, inner fibres pasted along the centre.

Tree-scars blaze the trail, the lightning's diameter and path,
those pulses resonate, sounding all around the globe.
They open you, they mark you deeply. After dark you see
lights shoot up from the top of thunderclouds, strange
    sprites.

This spring the tree's come into leaf, now the bark is healing,
hundreds of shoots emerge from the trunk. Four acorns
    grow
as the oak revives. Looks like it's the medium for the
    message,
the spark communicates directly; the wood can get wild with
    this.

# Also available from Polygon

## *The Powerlines*
## Gerrie Fellows

'This is a strong, even remarkable, piece of work ...'
Robert Crawford

*The Powerlines* chronicles the author's ancestors' emigration from Scotland to New Zealand – two small, geographically distant countries, united in this lyrical poetry collection which offers both a personal and a poetic encounter with history and place.

Through a sequence of linked poems and prose, and drawing on paintings, photographs and landscapes, *The Powerlines* presents the reader with a powerful, adventurous and technically accomplished collection which is emotionally charged, and filled with voices – the ancestral voices of family, childhood, women and emigrant Scots. Exploring and questioning identity, Fellows' poetry charts our ever-changing relationship to history, to the land and the changing environment, and to the transforming, and often destructive power of technology.

'A prose web in which every comma, every breath, is critical.'
*Product*

'*The Powerlines* by Gerrie Fellows is a striking book of poetry and prose which talks about the ancestral voices of her family's past in New Zealand and relationship with present-day Scotland and deserves a far wider audience.' Kathleen Jamie, *The Scotsman*

'This is a small book covering a big subject: two countries, two centuries and five generations. Fellows writes to everyone who shares an interest in what motivates people to change countries, and what happens to them when they do.' *North Words*

0 7486 6278 2
£7.99

Polygon
www.eup.ed.ac.uk

# Also available from Polygon

## *The Waistband and other poems*
## Donny O'Rourke

'What the book does show is a gifted poet set in a particular place
at a particular time and intensely aware of life both comic and
tragic: a poet without pomposity, a "man among men".'
Iain Crichton Smith

Donny O'Rourke's poetry has a jazzy, upbeat note to it, with the strains of Ireland
and America in the background. There are reflective poems on his parents, on
childhood, on being a man in the nineties, on food, on grief and renewal, and
losing weight (or not!).

O'Rourke's self-deprecating style is appealing, moving from one sensibility to the
next, and concerned with the acts of giving and receiving, transmitting culture,
ideas and thoughts. This is wide and generous poetry.

'This generous second collection shows he has gifts – a measure
of warmth, the confidence to speak plainly and clearly, and to
eulogise, always with a roguish humour to fall back on.'
*The List*

'The collection is an engaging read. Its poems are lively, accessible,
sometimes grievous or moving, often witty.'
*Scotland on Sunday*

0 7486 6232 4
£7.99

Polygon
www.eup.ed.ac.uk

**Also available from Polygon**

*Fax and other poems*
**Rody Gorman**

'This book marks the emergence of an energetic new voice.'
Robert Crawford

Rody Gorman's poems have an emotional power modulated by interruptions of sharp wit. This is a Gaelic poet who can move an audience with a poem about a fax machine as well as with a poem on walking boots.

He is at his strongest, however, when writing about love and most of this debut collection is given over to the modern idiom of love (as when he compares the image of a loved one coming back again and again like windscreen wipers).

'Rody Gorman's creative energies are running at full power in these poems, the language controlled, the imagery suble.'
Aonghas MacNeacail

'A writer of quality who manifestly has a gift for imagery and epigrammatic power.'
Iain Crichton Smith

0 7486 6216 2
£6.99

Polygon

www.eup.ed.ac.uk